T0197524

ANNA AND ZIG ZAG DAVE

KATHLEEN PERIC

WestBow Press books may be ordered through booksellers or by contacting:

WestBow Press
A Division of Thomas Nelson & Zondervan
1663 Liberty Drive
Bloomington, IN 47403
www.westbowpress.com
844.714.3454

Interior Image Credit: Kathleen Peric

ISBN: 978-1-6642-0414-0 (sc)
ISBN: 978-1-6642-0415-7 (e)

Library of Congress Control Number: 2020916768

Print information available on the last page.

WestBow Press rev. date: 9/8/2020

WESTBOW
PRESS®
A DIVISION OF THOMAS NELSON
& ZONDERVAN

This book is dedicated to my Granddaughter Annalise.

Kathleen Peric enjoys fun with her family dog
Dave. Dave is an older dog, but he is a lot of
fun for Anna and the whole family.

Anna and Zig Zag Dave..!

Anna found a dog in the pound named Dave.
She picked him because he did not misbehave!

Anna Got bored and took her new Beagle home to eat.

When she noticed his Zig Zag walk in his feet.

So Anna took Dave with her to bed to rest.
Because she thought that it was best!

Then Anna came up with a plan how to
make old Dave spark again!

Anna showed off Dave at the park.

But Dave her Beagle did not have a spark!

She put Dave on the slide to watch his eyes go wide!

She put Dave on the Merry Go Round
and swung it round and round!

Dave flew off and it only made him cough!

She pushed him as he walked, but it only
made his bones become stalked!

As Dave walked his ribs were out of place.
Dave for sure could not keep up pace!

And for sure he could not run in a race.

Anna thought she could fix him by letting him nap in the sun.

Maybe he can be more fun. But that did not work.

Because as he walked his bones began to jerk.

Anna showed him a bunny to chase. But
even then, he could not keep up pace.

Anna and Dave came across a Bee.

And found that he can hardly see!

Anna brought Dave to the zoo to see if
she could get rid of Dave's flu.

In the zoo Anna and Dave came across a parot,
but all Dave would do is just stare at it.

Anna and Dave came across a frog.
But all Dave would do is sit like a log.

Anna took Dave to see a shark, but
all he did was sit and park.

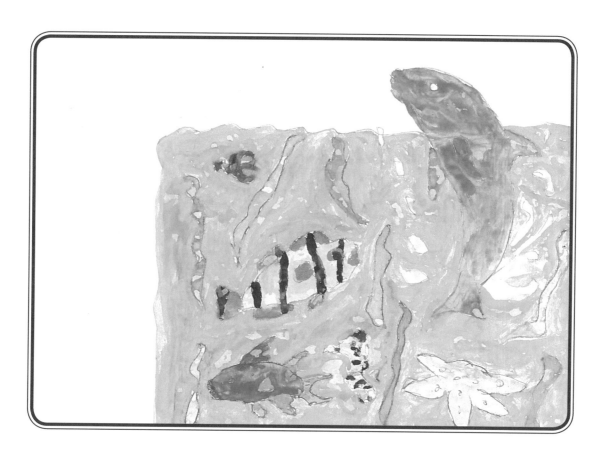

Anna took Dave to see the aquarium, but
all he did was sit and stare at them.

Anna took Dave to see a turtle, and she
still could not get him to hurdle.

At the zoo Anna brought Dave to see
a Duck a still Dave was stuck!

Anna brought Dave to see a horse, but
all he would do is sit of course!

Anna and Dave came

Across a cat, but he just sat!

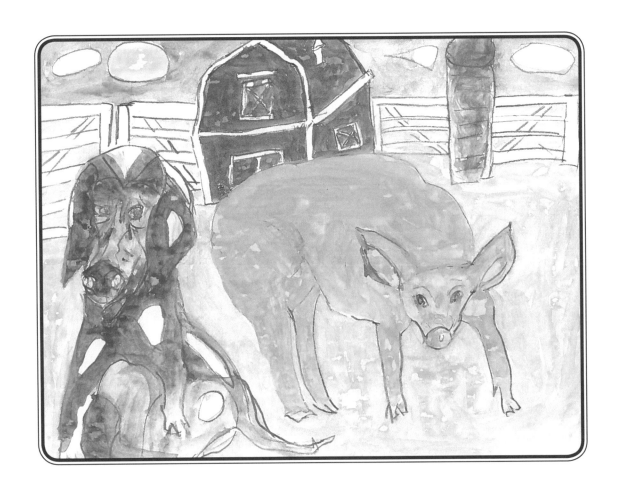

Anna brought Dave to see a pig, but
even the pig did not flip his wig!

Anna brought Dave home and shook her head.
Then Anna gave him a bone and put him to bed.

In the morning Zig Zag Dave jumped up out of bed.

He jumped down and fell from what she can tell.

Anna heard a thug and found Dave laying on the rug.

Zig Zag Dave wanted out. Because of the way he began to pout.

Zig Zag Dave got caught in the door!

Now Zig Zag Dave is Zig Zag no more!

Printed in the United States
By Bookmasters